For Mom—you are my sunshine! —S. M.

For Stanley, Emily, and Ellis—you are the sun
that keeps me filled with joy and life —S. L.

For Pluto—regardless of your status, you'll
always be part of my solar system —S.

Henry Holt and Company, *Publishers since 1866*

120 Broadway, New York, NY 10271 • mackids.com

Henry Holt® is a registered trademark of Macmillan Publishing Group, LLC

ISBN 978-1-250-19932-4

Library of Congress Control Number 2018936460

Our books may be purchased in bulk for promotional, educational, or business use.
Please contact your local bookseller or the Macmillan Corporate and Premium Sales Department
at (800) 221-7945 ext. 5442 or by e-mail at MacmillanSpecialMarkets@macmillan.com.

First edition, 2018 / Designed by April Ward

The artist used colored pencils and digital tools to create the illustrations in this book.

Printed in China by RR Donnelley, Dongguan City, Guangdong Province

9   10

OUR UNIVERSE

SUN!

ONE IN A BILLION

BY Sun (WITH STACY MCANULTY)

ILLUSTRATED BY Sun (AND STEVIE LEWIS)

Henry Holt and Company ✳ New York

Once upon a time—about
4.6 billion years ago—
a magnificent and important
star was born.

And that magnificent and important star was me.
Your Sun. (With a capital S.)

Yes, I am a STAR.

STAR: (1) a massive and luminous
ball of gas, full of energy;

(2) an outstandingly talented and popular performer.
I fit both definitions.

The Milky Way galaxy has over
100 billion stars.

ME!

That makes me one in a billion.
Or, um . . . one in 100 billion.

I'm not the biggest. *So what.*
Not the brightest. *Who cares.*
Not the oldest. *Whatever.*

But I am the most important.
At least to you Earthlings.

Can you hang out for eight minutes?
That's how long it takes my
light to reach Earth.

Yep, I give you heat and
light. *You're welcome.*

I'm so important that Earthlings should name a special day in my honor. We can call it Sundaaaa—oh, wait.

SUNDA

2

I'm famous for my heat and light, but I also hold our entire solar system together.

Scientists call it gravity.
What can I say?

The planets are attracted to me.

And because I'm the center of our solar system,
life revolves around me—literally.

SATURN

(Saturnian year =
10,756 Earth days)

NEPTUNE

(Neptunian year =
60,190 Earth days)

URANUS

(Uranian year =
30,687 Earth days)

SUN

VENUS

(Venusian year =
225 Earth days)

MERCURY

(Mercurial year =
88 Earth days)

EARTH

(Earth year =
365 Earth days)

MARS

(Martian year =
687 Earth days)

JUPITER

(Jovian year =
4,333 Earth days)

Look! They all go in the same direction.

Those other stars are far, far away from Earth.
Which makes them look teeny tiny and not so important.
I'm close—a mere 93 MiLLion miles from Earth.
To an Earthling, I look like this.

But to Neptunians, I'm 2,795 million
miles away. And I look like this.
(If there *were* Neptunians. There's
no known life on Neptune.)

Technically, I'm a yellow *dwarf* star.

IDENTIFICATION CARD

NAME: SUN
TYPE: DWARF STAR
DOB: LONG AGO

G2-MILKY WAY

PLASMA DONOR

But I'm still a big, big deal.

But you can't fill me with Earths because I'm hot stuff.
Compare:

A pizza oven:
700°F.

A hot
summer day:
90°F.

The orange-
yellow flames
in a campfire:
about 2,000°F.

Me!

°F

About 10,000°F on the surface. I can melt diamonds!

Me!

At my center, 27 million°F.

Ancient Earthlings thought I circled the Earth. *Can you imagine? Me revolving around Earth?*

JUPITER

SATURN

URANUS

VENUS

EARTH

MARS

MOON

NEPTUNE

MERCURY

SUN

And some might think that I sit in the sky all day and all night. *But I got moves, baby.* I'm spinning.

And because I'm not solid, my middle moves
faster than my top and bottom.

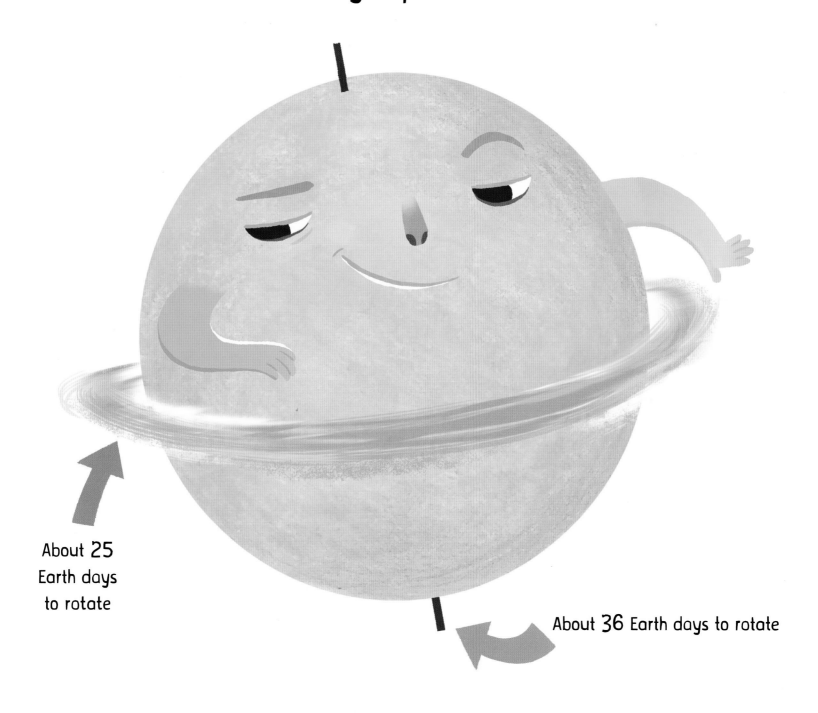

About 25
Earth days
to rotate

About 36 Earth days to rotate

Don't try this at home.

I'm not only important;
I'm generous *and* good looking.

Sunrises.

Sunsets.

Northern Lights.

Southern Lights.

Sit back and enjoy the show.

Sometimes, I like to be mysterious and sneak away for a few minutes. Solar eclipse! But don't worry, I'm just behind the Moon.

While I'm astronomically bigger than the Moon
(400 times wider), the Moon is astronomically
closer to Earth (almost 400 times closer).

My neighbor stars have fancy names.
Meet Proxima Centauri, Alpha Centauri A,
and Alpha Centauri B.

Me, I need just three letters.

Give me an S!

Give me a U!

Give me an N!

What does that spell? Sun!

Sun, Sun, he's our star. Light and heat from afar.

Please note: that's a capital S. I *am* important.

Not to hog the spotlight, but I've still got it.
I'm the same hot, bright star I've always been.

STARS FALL APART!!

...IBUNE

THE SOLAR NEW...

NEWS OF THE UNIVERSE

MELTDOW...

TOTAL CO...APSE

AL...

MILKY WAY HERALD

12 CEN

NEWS OF THE UNIVERSE

A stable star is a good star. You don't want your Sun getting hotter or cooling off. That would be really messy.

So grab your shades.

I plan to be in the biz for another five billion years.
You and me, we've got a bright future together.

Dear Reader,

I love our Sun, and I think he deserves a name. Perhaps Buck or Reginald or Mostest Importanus Centauri. Earth—our very own Planet Awesome—would not exist without Sun. And without Earth, there would be no chocolate chip cookies, picture books, or frisky puppies, which are a few of my favorite things. So I guess I need to say, Thank you, Sun (with a capital S)! Thank you for light, heat, energy, and the gravity that keeps Earth revolving at the most perfect distance from your superhot surface. Too close, we'd be scorched; too far away, we'd freeze. You're one in a billion.

With gratitude,

Stacy McAnulty

Author and frequent wearer of sunblock

P.S. Scientists are always making discoveries. As technology improves, we continue to learn more about our universe. Every attempt was made to bring you accurate numbers and facts. We checked, double-checked, and triple-dog checked. So in the future, if you hear that an astrophysicist has better information, feel free to write in this book . . . unless you borrow the book from a friend or a library. Then just write down the new data on a sticky note and put it inside. Thanks!

Q&A with the Star* of Our Book, Sun

*Get it? Star of our book?

Q: Who is your favorite planet? And remember, this book will be read mostly by Earthlings.

A: Of course I don't have a favorite. Each is special—and kind of puny. By mass, I make up 99.8 percent of the entire solar system. That's like asking a human to select a favorite fingernail.

Q: You've been around for nearly 4.6 billion years and are expected to shine at least another five billion more. How do you stay so enthusiastic?

A: I like to keep moving. As you have read, I rotate. But also, about every 11 years, my poles change magnetic polarity. Positive becomes negative, and negative becomes positive. This causes impressive solar storms. I also orbit the Milky Way—taking Earth and all my planets with me. That's a long trip—about 230 million years.

Q: From the outside, you look like a giant, fiery ball. But what are you really made of?

A: Mostly hydrogen and some helium.

Q: When young Earth artists draw you in a picture, what color do you prefer?

A: Technically, I'm a yellow dwarf. From space, with no atmosphere in the way, I'm basically white. But without me, Earthlings wouldn't see any colors—it'd be too dark. So use any crayon; I don't mind. I would recommend adding glitter to any picture to capture my sparkling personality.

Q: Last question—do you have any advice for readers?

A: Yes. Never stare directly at me—even during a solar eclipse—because I can damage your eyes. You delicate

SUN by the Numbers

Age: Scientists estimate Sun's age between 4.5 and 4.6 billion years old. That would be a lot of candles on his cake.

Radius: Radius is the distance from the center of a circle or sphere to the edge.

Sun's radius = 432,169 miles

Earth's radius = 3,959 miles

Moon's radius = 1,080 miles

Mass and Volume: Mass is the amount of material an object contains. Volume is the amount of space an object takes up. A balloon filled with air and a balloon filled with water would have the same volume, but the balloon filled with water would have more mass. And a balloon filled with water is more fun.

Sun's mass = $1,988,500 \times 10^{24}$ kg

Earth's mass = 5.9724×10^{24} kg

By mass, Sun is 333,000 times bigger than Earth.

Sun's volume = $1,412,000 \times 10^{12}$ km^3

Earth's volume = 1.083×10^{12} km^3

By volume, Sun is 1,304,000 times bigger than Earth.

Distance: The distance between Earth and Sun actually changes because Earth's orbit is not a perfect circle. It's more of an oval.

On average, Earth is 92.96 million miles from Sun. We also say Earth and Sun are one astronomical unit (1 AU) apart.

Distance from Sun:

Mercury = 0.4 AU	Saturn = 9.5 AU
Venus = 0.7 AU	Uranus = 19 AU
Mars = 1.5 AU	Neptune = 30 AU
Jupiter = 5.2 AU	Pluto (Not a planet!) = 39.5 AU

Composition: Astronomers say there are 67 elements in Sun, mostly hydrogen and helium.

Hydrogen atoms = 91.2%

Helium atoms = 8.7%

Other atoms = 0.1%

Atoms are the teeny tiny building blocks that make up all materials.

Our Solar System:

One star (Our Sun!)

Eight planets

Five dwarf planets (including poor Pluto)

At least 157 moons

Hundreds of thousands of asteroids, comets, and meteors

One You (which makes you important too!)

Sources

Dunford, Bill, and Celeste Hoang. "Our Solar System: Our Galactic Neighborhood." NASA Science. Updated Jan. 25, 2018. solarsystem.nasa.gov/solar-system/our-solar-system/overview/.

——. "Sun: Our Star." NASA Science. Updated Jan. 25, 2018. solarsystem.nasa.gov/solar-system/sun/overview/.

Goldsmith, Mike, Margaret Hynes, and Barbara Taylor. *Earth and Space: A Thrilling Adventure from Planet Earth into the Universe.* New York: Kingfisher, 2016.

Kerrod, Robin. *Eyewitness Universe.* New York: DK Publishing, 2015.

Sharp, Tim. "What Is the Sun Made Of?" Nov. 3, 2017. space.com/17170-what-is-the-sun-made-of.html.

Trefil, James. *Space Atlas: Mapping the Universe and Beyond.* Washington, DC: National Geographic, 2012.

Williams, David R. "Sun Fact Sheet." NASA Space Science Data Coordinated Archive. Updated Dec. 16, 2016. nssdc.gsfc.nasa.gov/planetary/factsheet/sunfact.html.

Young, C. Alex. "The Sun's Magnetic Poles Have Flipped . . . Solar Max Is Here!" Feb. 3, 2014. thesuntoday.org/solar-facts/suns-magnetic-poles-flipped-solar-max-is-here/.